The New
Guitar Songbook

Also by F.M. Noad

Playing the Guitar
Solo Guitar Playing, Book One
Solo Guitar Playing, Book Two

The New Guitar Songbook

Frederick M. Noad

Schirmer Books
A Division of Macmillan, Inc.
NEW YORK

Collier Macmillan Publishers
LONDON

SCHIRMER BOOKS
A Division of Macmillan, Inc.
866 Third Avenue, New York, N.Y. 10022

Collier Macmillan Canada, Inc.

Library of Congress Catalog Card Number : 85-750512

Printed in the United States of America

printing number
1   2   3   4   5   6   7   8   9   10

Grateful acknowledgment is made to those publishers listed below who have given permission
    for copyrighted works to be used as a basis for the guitar versions.

"Coventry Carol," version of Martin Shaw, by permission of A. R. Mowbray and Co., Oxford.
"Down in Yon Forest," melody and text collected by Ralph Vaughan Williams, by permission
    of Stainer and Bell Ltd., Reigate.
"Lute Book Lullaby," from the version in the *Oxford Book of Carols*, by permission of
    Oxford University Press.
"Zorongo," words by Federico Garcia Lorca, by permission of Editorial Losada S.A., Buenos
    Aires and Isabel Garcia Lorca.
"Pierrot's Song," copyright 1913 by Oliphant Down. Copyright 1941, in renewal, by Alice Down.
"Down By the Salley Gardens," from *Collected Poems* by W. B. Yeats, by permission of Mr.
    M. B. Yeats, Anne Yeats, and Macmillan & Co., Ltd., London.
"All Through the Night," words by Harold Boulton and printed by permission of Messrs. J.B.
    Cramer and Company, Ltd., London.
"Abschied," translation by Anne Goodrich Heck from *Mauro Giuliani, Sechs Lieder Op. 89* by
    permission of Tecla Editions, Preachers' Court, Charterhouse, London EC1M 6AS.
"The Constant Lover," © 1985 by Peter Heneker. Used by permission.

Library of Congress Cataloging in Publication Data
Main entry under title:

The new guitar songbook.

    Popular, folk, traditional, and art songs,
including Christmas carols, with acc. arr. for guitar.
    Rev. ed. of: The Guitar songbook.
    1. Songs with guitar.   2. Music, Popular (Songs, etc.)
3. Folk-songs, English.   4. Carols, English.   I. Noad,
Frederick M.   II. Guitar songbook.
M1623.N48 1985   85–750512
ISBN 0–02–872140–3

Contents

Acknowledgments

My most grateful thanks to Howard Heitmeyer
for his constant help in the preparation of this manuscript,
to Gloria Maxson for very helpful suggestions and encouragement,
and to Brita and Ryno Edeborg for invaluable help
in translating the Swedish lyrics of Carl Michael Bellman.

—F.N.

Introduction

The first proposed title for this collection, when it was in preparation in the late sixties, was *The Family Guitar Songbook*. The object was to assemble a number of well loved folk and traditional songs with very simple guitar accompaniments that would be within the range of the average amateur, and thus provide a basic book for use in homes where the guitar rather than the piano was the domestic instrument. The first section of the current publication corresponds to that original format, offering 30 songs chosen mainly from the British-American heritage. A few Christmas Carols of a type suitable for accompaniment by the guitar were also added. However, even in the first edition, published as *The Guitar Songbook*, it was decided to go further and to add some more musically complete works because of the shortage of published repertoire in this area.

For many centuries now the plucked strings have been used with particular success to accompany the voice. In the sixteenth century the French "Air de Cour" and the English Ayre both favored the lute, while in Spain the *vihuela*, a forerunner of the modern guitar, was widely used to accompany the solo voice. At the beginning of the seventeenth century Caccini's *Le Nuove Musiche*, a collection of solo songs performed by him to a large (theorbo) lute, set the stage for an era of highly expressive song fitted more closely to the poetry than the music of the polyphonic era. An example, "Belle Rose Porporine," is included in this collection. In the first half of the nineteenth century, when the guitar with an extra sixth string emerged as an instrument of great popularity, it was common for songs to be published with both guitar and pianoforte accompaniments. Unfortunately, today song publications with complete guitar arrangements are rare, and too often even popular music that has originally been played with guitar accompaniment appears on the market scored for the keyboard with only chord symbols for the guitar. In the face of this shortage of material it becomes irresistible to offer some of the treasures of the past.

For *The New Guitar Songbook* I have included a number of songs suitable for concert performance on any level. From Spain, "Si La Noce

Haze Escura," an anonymous Villancico from the early part of the sixteenth century, has a musical perfection that translates very naturally to the guitar and voice arrangement. I have followed the style of the contemporary "vihuelistas" in preserving the vocal lines. "Tant Que Vivray" by Sermisy was highly popular tune at about the same period in France, and appeared in many collections. Like "Greensleeves," its catchy tune seems in no way dated. From England "Come Sorrow Come" of Morley and "I Saw My Lady Weep" by Dowland reflect with exceptional poignancy the Elizabethan melancholy, while Campion's delightful "It Fell on a Summer's Day" shows the other side of the picture. Purcell's "Strike the Viol" is from his book *Orpheus Brittanicus* (1695), while the rival collection *Amphion Anglicus* (1698) of John Blow is represented by "The Self-Banished." From Ireland two poems of Thomas Moore set to traditional tunes are added to "Believe Me If All Those Endearing Young Charms." The guitar settings are by the most famous guitar figure in nineteenth-century England, the virtuoso Catherina Pelzer, later Madame Sydney Pratten. From Vienna Schubert's "Ungeduld" from *Die Schöne Müllerin* and Giuliani's "Abschied" are examples of music published with both guitar and pianoforte accompaniments.

The heritage of Carl Michael Bellman is a national treasure to the people of Sweden. This seventeenth-century troubador wrote wonderfully irreverent poetry that he sang to the theorbo lute, composing some tunes and adapting others to his use. His "Song at Nightfall" is a real gem that I am happy to include.

Modern settings of older poetry are represented by Peter Heneker's version of Suckling's "Constant Lover," and my own setting of "Sigh No More, Ladies" from Shakespeare's *Much Ado About Nothing*.

The overall choice is of course purely personal; but these are songs that have given me a great deal of pleasure, which I hope to share by means of this book.

Popular, Folk, and Traditional Songs

All Through the Night

Sir Harold Boulton (1859–1935)

Traditional (Welsh)

Sleep my child, let peace at-tend thee, All through the night.

Guard - ian an - gels God will send thee, All through the night.

Soft the drow - sy hours are creep-ing, hill and vale in slum - ber steep-ing,

I my lov - ing vig - il keep-ing, All through the night.

While the moon her watch is keeping,
All through the night,
While the weary world is sleeping,
All through the night.

O'er thy spirit gently stealing,
Visions of delight revealing,
Breathes a pure and holy feeling,
All through the night.

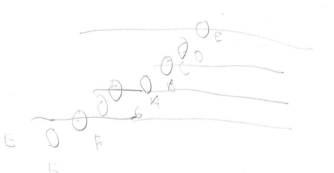

Annie Laurie

William Douglas of Fingland (c. 1800)

Lady John Douglas Scott (1810–1900)

Her brow is like the snowdrift,
Her throat is like the swan,
Her face it is the fairest,
That e'er the sun shone on;
That e'er the sun shone on,
And dark blue is her e'e,
And for Bonnie Annie Laurie,
I'd lay me doon and dee.

The Ash Grove

Traditional (Welsh)

6

dear one, The joy of my heart; A - round us for glad - ness, The blue - bells were ring - ing, Ah, then lit - tle___ thought I How soon we should part.

Still glows the bright sunshine,
O'er valley and mountain,
Still warbles the blackbird,
His note from the tree.
Still trembles the moonbeam
On streamlet and fountain,
But what are the beauties
Of nature to me.
With sorrow deep sorrow
My bosom is laden,
All day I go mourning
In search of my love.
Ye echoes, oh tell me,
Where is the sweet maiden?
She sleeps 'neath the green turf
Down by the ash grove.

Aura Lee

W. W. Fosdick

George R. Poulton

As the black-bird in the spring, 'Neath the wil-low tree,____

Sat and piped, I heard him sing, sing of Au - ra Lee.

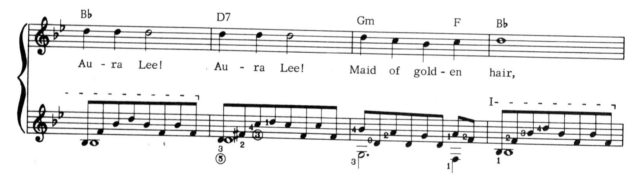

Au - ra Lee! Au - ra Lee! Maid of gold - en hair,

Sun - shine came a - long with thee, And swal-lows in the air.

On her cheek the rose was born,
'Twas music when she spoke,
In her eyes the rays of morn,
With sudden splendor broke.

Aura Lee! Aura Lee!
Maid of golden hair,
Sunshine came along with thee,
And swallows in the air.

Barbara Allen

He sent his man unto her then,
To the town where she was dwellin';
You must come to my master dear,
If your name be Barbara Allen.

For death is printed on his face,
And o'er his heart is stealin';
Then haste away to comfort him,
O lovely Barbara Allen.

Though death be printed on his face,
And o'er his heart is stealin',
Yet little better shall he be,
For bonnie Barbara Allen.

So slowly, slowly, she came up,
And slowly she came nigh him,
And all she said, when there she came,
Young man I think you're dying.

He turned his face unto her straight,
With deadly sorrow sighing;
O lovely maid, come pity me,
I'm on my deathbed lying.

If on your deathbed you do lie,
What needs the tale your tellin',
I cannot keep you from your death;
Farewell, said Barbara Allen.

When he was dead and laid in grave,
Her heart was struck with sorrow,
O mother, mother, make my bed,
For I shall die tomorrow.

Hard-hearted creature him to slight,
Who loved me so dearly;
O that I'd been more kind to him,
When he was alive and near me!

She, on her deathbed as she lay,
Begg'd to be buried by him;
And sore repented of the day,
That she did e'er deny him.

Farewell, she said, ye virgins all,
And shun the fault I fell in;
Henceforth take warning by the fall
Of cruel Barbara Allen.

Believe Me if All Those Endearing Young Charms

Thomas Moore (1779–1852)

Traditional Irish Air (My Lodging is on the Cold Ground)

Be - lieve me if all those en - dear-ing young charms, Which I gaze on so fond - ly to - day,_____ Were to change by to - mor - row, and fleet in my arms, Like fair - y gifts fad - ing a - way;_____ Thou wouldst still be a-dored as this mo - ment thou art, Let thy lov - li-ness fade as it

It is not while beauty and youth are
    thine own,
And thy cheeks unprofaned by a tear,
That the fervour and faith of a soul can
    be known,
To which time will but make thee more dear.
No, the heart that has truly loved never
    forgets,
But as truly loves on to the close;
As the sunflower turns on her God when
    he sets,
The same look which she turned when
    he rose.

The Blue Bells of Scotland

Attributed to Mrs. Jordan (c. 1800)

14

O where, and O where, did your highland
 laddie dwell?
O where, and O where, did your highland
 laddie dwell?
He dwelt in bonnie Scotland, where blooms
 the sweet Bluebell,
And it's O in my heart that I love my
 laddie well!

O what, and O what, does your highland
 laddie wear?
O what, and O what, does your highland
 laddie wear?
A bonnet with a lofty plume and on his breast
 a plaid,
And it's O in my heart, I love my highland lad!

The Bonny Earl of Moray

Traditional (Scottish)

Ye Hie-lands and ye Low-lands,— O where hae ye been? They hae

slain the Earl of Mo-ray,— And laid him on the green. He was a braw

gal-lant, And he rade at the ring; And the bon-nie Earl of Mo-ray,— He

might hae been a king, O lang will his la - dy look, Frae the Cas-tle

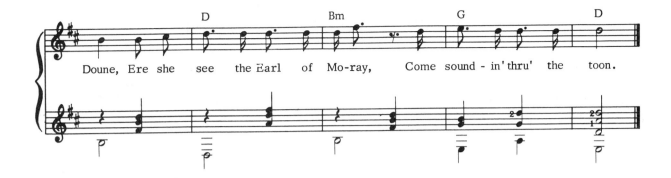

Doune, Ere she see the Earl of Mo-ray, Come sound - in' thru' the toon.

O wae tae ye, Huntley,
And wherefore did ye sae?
I bade ye bring him wi' ye
And forbade ye him to slay.
He was a braw gallant,
And he played at the glove;
And the bonny Earl of Moray,
He was the Queen's love!
O lang will his lady
Look frae the Castle Doune,
Ere she see the Earl of Moray
Come soundin' thru' the toon.

Down in Yon Forest

Traditional (English)

At the bedside there lies a stone:
The bells of paradise, I heard them ring:
Which the sweet virgin Mary knelt upon:
And I love my lord Jesus above anything.

Under the bed there runs a flood:
The bells of paradise, I heard them ring:
The one half runs water, the other runs blood:
And I love my lord Jesus above anything.

At the bed's foot there grows a thorn:
The bells of paradise, I heard them ring:
Whichever blows blossom since he was born:
And I love my lord Jesus above anything.

Over that bed the moon shines bright:
The bells of paradise, I heard them ring:
Denoting our savior was born this night:
And I love my lord Jesus above anything.

Drink to Me only with Thine Eyes

Ben Jonson (1616)

Music ascribed to Capt. Mellish

Drink to me on - ly with__ thine eyes__ and I__ will pledge with

mine; Or leave a kiss with - in__ the cup,__ and I'll__ not ask for

wine;_____ The thirst__ that from the soul__ doth rise, doth

ask a drink di - vine_____ But might I of Jove's

nec - tar sip__ I would__ not change for thine.

I sent thee late a rosy wreath, not so much
    honoring thee,
As giving it a hope that there it could not
    withered be;
But thou thereon didst only breathe, and
    sent'st it back to me,
Since when it grows and smells, I swear, not
    of itself but thee.

Early One Morning

Traditional (English)

Early one morn - ing, Just as the sun was ris - ing, I heard a maid sing___ in the val - ley be - low,

Refrain

"O don't de - ceive___ me, O nev - er leave___ me, How___ could you use___ a___ poor___ maid - en so?"

Remember the vows that you made to your
  Mary;
Remember the bow'r where you vow'd to
  be true.
O, don't deceive me etc.

O gay is the garland, and fresh are the roses
I've culled from the garden to bind on
  your brow.
O, don't deceive me etc.

Thus sung the maiden her sorrows bewailing,
Thus sung the poor maid in the valley below.
O, don't deceive me etc.

Flow Gently Sweet Afton

Robert Burns

James Spilman (1812–1896)

Flow gent - ly sweet Af - ton A - mong thy green braes; Flow gent - ly, I'll sing thee A song in thy praise; My Mar - y's a - sleep By thy mur - mur - ing stream, Flow gent - ly sweet Af - ton, Dis - turb not her dreams. Thou__ stock - dove, who's ech - o Re - sounds through the glen, Ye__ wild whist - ling black - birds In yon__ thorn - y__

den,   Thou   green   crest - ed_____   lap - wing,   The   scream - ing   for -

bear,   I   charge you   dis - turb   not   my   slum - ber - ing   fair.

How pleasant thy banks and
Green valleys below,
Where wild in the woodlands,
The primroses blow,
There oft, as mild evening
Weeps over the lea,
The sweet scented birk
Shades my Mary and me.

Thou stockdove, who's echo
Resounds through the glen,
Ye wild whistling blackbirds
In yon thorny den,
Thou green crested lapwing
The screaming forbear,
I charge you disturb not
My slumbering fair.

The Golden Vanity

Traditional

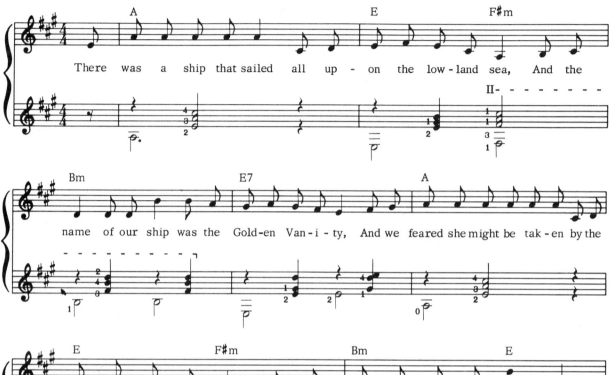

There was a ship that sailed all up - on the low-land sea, And the

name of our ship was the Gold-en Van-i - ty, And we feared she might be tak - en by the

Span - ish en - e - my, As we sailed up - on the low - land,

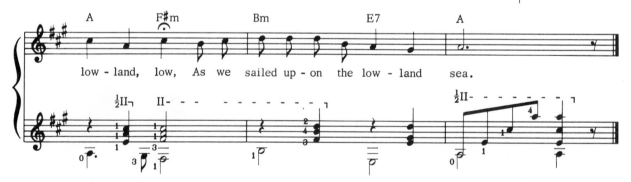

low - land, low, As we sailed up-on the low - land sea.

Then up stepped our cabin boy and boldly out
  spoke he,
And he said to the captain, "What will you
  give to me,
If I swim alongside of the Spanish enemy,
And sink her in the lowland, lowland, low,
And sink her in the lowland sea."

"O I will give you silver, and I will give you
  gold,
And my own fair daughter your bonny bride
  shall be,
If you swim alongside of the Spanish enemy,
And sink her in the lowland, lowland, low,
And sink her in the lowland sea."

The boy made himself ready, and overboard
  sprang he,
And he swam alongside of the Spanish enemy,
And with his auger sharp in her side he bored
  holes three,
And sank her in the lowland, lowland, low,
And sank her in the lowland sea.

Then the boy turned around, and back again
  swam he,
And he cried out to the skipper of the Golden
  Vanity,
But the skipper would not listen, for his word
  he did not heed;
And he left him in the lowland, lowland, low,
And he left him in the lowland sea.

The boy then swam around, and he came to
  the portside,
And he looked up to his messmates, and
  bitterly he cried,
"O messmates haul me up, for I'm drifting
  with the tide,
And I'm sinking in the lowland, lowland, low,
And I'm sinking in the lowland sea."

His messmates took him up, and on the deck
  he died,
And they sewed him in his hammock that was
  so fair and wide,
And they lower'd him over gently, and he
  drifted with the tide,
And he sank in the lowland, lowland, low,
And he sank in the lowland sea.

Greensleeves

heart of gold,____And who but my la - dy Green - sleeves.

I have been ready at your hand,
To grant whatever you would crave;
I have both waged life and land,
Your love and goodwill for to have.

Refrain:
Greensleeves was all my joy,
Greensleeves was my delight;
Greensleeves was my heart of gold,
And who but my Lady Greensleeves?

I bought thee kerchers to thy head
That were wrought fine and gallantly;
I kept thee both at board and bed,
Which cost my purse well favouredly.

Thy gown was of the grassy green,
Thy sleeves of satin hanging by,
Which made thee be our harvest queen,
And yet thou wouldst not love me.

Well, I will pray to God on high,
That thou my constancy mayst see,
And that yet once before I die,
Thou will vouchsafe to love me.

The Harp that Once Thro' Tara's Halls

Thomas Moore
                                          Traditional Irish Air ("Molly My Treasure")

Guitar arrangement by Catharina Josepha Pratten (1821–1895).

½V

No more to Chiefs and La - dies bright The
harp of Ta - ra swells; The chord, a - lone that breaks at night, Its
tale of ru - in tells: Thus Free - dom now so sel - dom wakes, The
on - ly throb she gives, Is when some heart in - dig - nant breaks, To
show that still she loves! _____

How Should I Your True Love Know?

William Shakespeare　　　　　　　　　　　　　　　　　　　　　　　　*Anonymous*

1. How should I your true love know From an-oth - er one?

By his cock - le hat and staff And his san - dal shoon.

1. He is dead and gone la - dy, He is dead and gone;
2. White his shroud as the moun-tain snow Lard - ed with sweet flow'rs;

At his head a grass-green turf, At his heels a stone.
Which be - wept to the grave did go With true love show - ers.

The Meeting of the Waters

Thomas Moore

Traditional Irish Air ("The Old Head of Dennis")

1. There is not in the wide world a val - ley so sweet As that
2. Yet it was not that na - ture had shed o'er the scene Her ___

vale in whose bo - som the bright wa - ters meet. Oh! the last rays of _ feel - ing and
pu rest of _ crys - tal and bright-est of green; 'Twas _ not the soft _ ma - gic of

life must de - part, Ere the bloom of that val - ley shall fade from my heart; Ere the
stream - let or hill; Oh! _ no it was some -thing more ex - qui - site still: Oh! _

Guitar arrangement by Catharina Josepha Pratten (1821–1895).

33

bloom of that val - ley shall fade from my heart!
no it was something more ex - qui - site still:

3. 'Twas that friends, the be - lov'd of my bo - som were near, Who made
4. Sweet__ vale of A - vo - ca! how calm could I rest In thy

ev' - ry dear scene of en - chant - ment more dear; And who felt how the best charms of
bo - som of shade, with the friends I love best, Where the storms, which we feel in this

na - ture im - prove When we see them re - flect - ed from
cold world should cease, And our hearts, like thy wa - ters, be

looks   that   we   love.   When we   see   them re -   flect - ed   from

min - gled   in   peace!   And our   hearts,   like thy   wa - ters   be

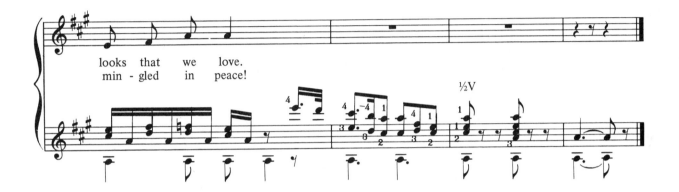

looks   that   we   love.

min - gled   in   peace!

The Minstrel Boy

Thomas Moore

Irish air ("The Moreen")

The min-strel boy__ to the war is gone, In the ranks of death__ you'll find__ him; His fa-ther's sword he has gird-ed on, And his wild harp slung__ be-hind him. "O land of song," said the war-rior bard, "Though all the world be-trays__ thee, One sword at least, thy__ rights shall guard, one faith-ful harp shall praise thee.

The minstrel fell, but the foeman's chain
Could not bring that proud soul under;
The harp he loved ne'er spoke again,
For he tore its chords asunder;
And said, "No, chain shall sulley thee,
Thou soul of love and bravery
Thy songs were made for the pure and free,
They shall never sound in Slav'ry.

Nobody Knows the Trouble I've Seen

Negro Spiritual

Refrain:
Nobody knows the trouble I've seen,
Nobody knows but Jesus.
Nobody knows the trouble I've seen,
Glory hallelujah!

Although you see me goin' on so,
Oh, yes, Lord;
I have my trials here below,
Oh, yes, Lord.

I never shall forget that day,
Oh, yes, Lord;
When Jesus washed my sins away,
Oh, yes, Lord.

Oh, No John, No

Traditional

On yon-der hill there stands a—maid-en, Who she is I do not—know,

I'll go—court her for her—beau-ty; She must an-swer yes or no.

Oh, no, John, no, John, no,—John, no. 2. My fa-ther was a Span-ish cap-tain,

Went to sea a year a-go, First he—kissed me, then he—left me;

Bade me al-ways an-swer no. Oh, no, John, no, John, no,—John, no.

3. Oh madam, in your face is beauty,
On your lips red roses grow,
Will you take me for your lover?
Madam, answer yes or no.

Oh, no, John, no, John, no John, no.

4. Oh madam, since you are so cruel,
And you wish to scorn me so,
If I may not be your lover,
Madam, will you let me go?

Oh, no, John, no, John, no John, no.

5. Oh hark, I hear the Church bells ringing,
Will you come and be my wife?
Or, dear madam, have you settled
To live single all your life?

Oh, no, John, no, John, no John, no!

Old Paint

Traditional (American)

I ride an old paint,__ And I lead an old Dan,__ I'm goin' to Mon-tan-a, To

throw the hou-li-han. They feed in the cou-lees, They wa - ter in the draw, Their

tails are all mat-ted,__ Their backs are all raw; Ride a - round lit-tle do-gies, Ride a-

round__ re-al slow, For the fier - y and the snuff-y__ Are ra-rin' to go.

Old Bill Jones had two daughters and a song,
One went to Denver and the other
    went wrong,
His wife she died in a poolroom fight,
But still he keeps singin' from morning
    'til night.

Refrain:
Ride around little dogies,
Ride around real slow,
For the fiery and the snuffy
Are rarin' to go.

When I die take my saddle from the wall,
Put it on my Pony, lead him out of his stall,
Tie my bones to his back, turn our faces to
    the West,
And we'll ride the prairie that we love
    the best.
Ride around little dogies etc.

The Riddle Song

Traditional

I gave my love a cher-ry that has no stone, I gave my love a chick-en that has no bone, I gave my love a sto-ry that has no end, I gave my love a ba-by with no cry - en.

How can there be a cherry that has no stone?
How can there be a chicken that has no bone?
How can there be a story that has no end?
How can there be a baby with no cry-en?

A cherry when it's blooming, it has no stone,
A chicken when it's pipin', it has no bone,
The story of I love you, it has no end,
And a baby when it's sleeping, there's no cryen.

The Salley Gardens

W. B. Yeats (1865–1939)

Irish Tune

It was down by the Sal - ley gar - dens, My love and I did meet. She passed the Sal - ley gar - dens, On lit - tle snow - white feet. She bid me take love eas - y, As the leaves grow on the tree, But I be - ing young and

fool - ish, With her did not a - gree.

In a field by the river,
My love and I did stand,
And on my leaning shoulder,
She placed her snow white hand;

She bid me take life easy,
As the grass grows on the weirs,
But I was young and foolish,
And now am full of tears.

Shenandoah

Traditional (American)

O Shenandoah, I love your daughter,
Away, you rolling river:
I'll take her 'cross your roaring water,
Away, I'm bound away, 'cross the wide
  Missouri.

O Shenandoah, I'm bound to leave you,
Away, you rolling river:
O Shenandoah, I'll not deceive you,
Away, I'm bound away, 'cross the wide
  Missouri.

48

Soldiers Three

Traditional (English)

Chorus:
We be soldiers three,
Pardonnez-moi, je vous en prie,
Lately come forth of the low country,
With never a penny of money.

And he that will not pledge me this,
Pardonnez-moi, je vous en prie,
Pays for the shot whatever it is,
With never a penny of money.

Charge it again boys, charge it again,
Pardonnez-moi, je vous en prie,
As long as you have any ink in your pen,
With never a penny of money.

The Tavern in the Town

Traditional (English)

There is a tav-ern in the town, in the town,

Where my true love sits him down, sits him down,__ And__ drinks his

wine 'mid laugh-ter__ free, And nev - er, nev-er thinks of

me, thinks of me! Fare thee well for I must leave thee, Do not let this part-ing

grieve me, But re - mem-ber that the best of friends must part, must part, A -

He left me for a damsel dark, damsel dark,
Each Friday night they used to spark, used
    to spark,
And now my love once true to me,
Takes that dark damsel on his knee, on
    his knee!

Chorus:

Fare thee well for I must leave thee,
Do not let this parting grieve me,
But remember that the best of friends must
    part, must part.
Adieu, adieu, kind friends adieu, kind friends
    adieu,
I can no longer stay with you, stay with you,
I'll hang my harp on a weeping willow tree.
And may the world go well with thee, well
    with thee.

Venezuela

Sea Chanty

I met her in Ven-e-zu-e - - la,_____ With a
bas - ket on her head, If she loved oth-ers,_
she did-n't say, But I knew she'd do to pass a - way, To
pass_ a - way_ the time in Ven-e-zu-e - - la, To
pass_ a - way_ the time_ in Ven-e-zu-e - - la._

I bought her a beautiful sash of blue,
A beautiful sash of blue,
Because I knew what she would do,
With all the tricks I knew she knew,
To pass away the time in Venezuela,
To pass away the time in Venezuela.

And then the wind was out to sea,
The wind was out to sea,
And she was taking leave of me,
I said, "Cheer up there'll always be,
Sailors on leave ashore in Venezuela,
Sailors on leave ashore in Venezuela.

Waly Waly

Based on version collected by Cecil Sharp

Traditional

The wa-ter is wide I can not get o'er, And nei-ther have I wings to fly, Give me a— boat that will car-ry— two, And both shall row my true love and— I. O, down in the mead-ow the oth-er day, A-gath'ring flow'rs so fine and gay, A-gath-er-ing flow - ers both red and— blue, I lit - tle thought what false love can— do.

54

I leaned my back up against some oak,
Thinking that he was trusty tree,
But first he bended and then he broke,
And so did my false love to me.

Refrain:
O, down in the meadow the other day,
A-gath'ring flow'rs so fine and gay,
A-gathering flowers both red and blue,
I little thought what false love can do.

I put my hand into some soft bed,
Thinking the sweetest flower to find,
I pricked my finger till it bled,
And left the sweetest flower behind.

O love is handsome, and love is fine,
And love's a jewel when it is new;
But when it is old, it groweth cold,
And fades away like morning dew.

Reprinted by permission of Novello and Company, Ltd.

Will Ye No' Come Back Again

Lady Nairne (1766–1845)

Finlay Dun

Bon - nie Char-lie's gone a - wa', Safe - ly o'er the friend - ly main,

Man - y a heart will break in twa, Should he no' come back a - gain.

Will ye no' come back a - gain? Will ye no' come back a - gain?

Bet - ter loved ye can - na' be, Will ye no' come back a - gain?

Many a traitor 'mang the isles,
Break the band o' nature's law;
Many a traitor wi' his wiles,
Sought to wear his life awa'.

Chorus:
Will ye no' come back again?
Will ye no' come back again?
Better loved ye canna' be,
Will ye no' come back again?

Many a gallant soldier fought,
Many a gallant chief did fa',
Death itself were dearly bought,
All for Scotland's king and law.

Sweet the lav' rocks note and lang,
Lilting wildly up the glen;
And aye the o'erword o' the sang,
Will ye no' come back again?

Zorongo

F. Garcia Lorca

Traditional

Translation

The hands of my affection
Are embroidering a cape
With tiny silken wallflowers
And with little droplets of rain.

When you were betrothed to me
In the white springtime,
The hooves of your horse
Were as four cries of silver.

The moon is a tiny well,
And the flowers now mean nothing.
All that matters are your arms
When in the night you hold me.

Translation by M.C. Noad.

Christmas Carols

Coventry Carol

Based on version by Martin Shaw

15th Century Carol

Not too slow

Refrain

Lul - ly, lul - la, thou lit - tle ti - ny child, By by lul -

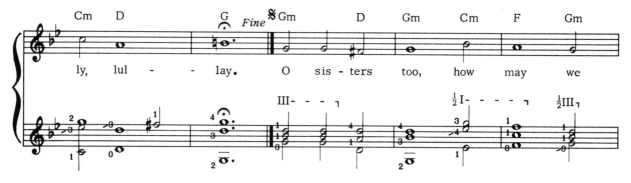

ly, lul - - lay. O sis - ters too, how may we

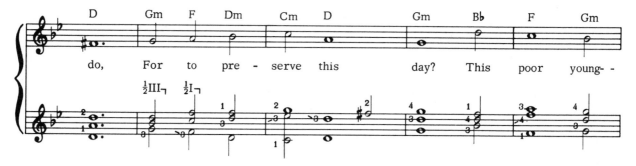

do, For to pre - serve this day? This poor young- -

ling, — For whom we do sing, By by lul - ly lu - - lay.

After 3rd verse sing Refrain again.

62

Herod, the king, in his raging,
Charged he hath this day,
His men of might,
In his own sight,
All young children to slay.

That woe is me, poor child for thee,
And ever morn and day.
For thy parting neither say nor sing
By by lully, lullay.

Refrain:
Lully, lulla, thou little tiny child,
By by lully, lullay.

The First Nowell

Traditional

The first Now - ell, the an - gel did say, Was to cer - tain poor shep - herds in fields as they lay; In fields where they lay keep - ing their sheep, On a cold win - ter's night that was so deep.

Refrain

Now - ell, Now - ell, Now - ell, Now - ell,

64

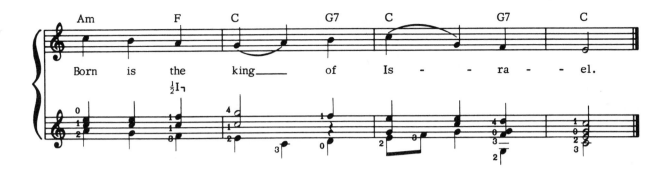

Born is the king of Is - ra - el.

They looked up and saw a star,
Shining in the east, beyond them far,
And to the earth it gave great light,
And so it continued both day and night.

Refrain:
Nowell, Nowell, Nowell, Nowell,
Born is the king of Israel.

And by the light of that same star
Three wise men came from wandering far;
To seek for a king was their intent,
And to follow the star wherever it went.

This star drew nigh to the northwest,
O'er Bethlehem it took its rest,
And there it did both stop and stay,
Right over the place where Jesus lay.

Then entered in those wise men three,
Full reverently upon their knee,
And offered there, in his presence,
Their gold and myrrh and frankincense.

The Holly and the Ivy

Traditional (English)

The hol-ly and the i-vy, When they are both full grown, Of all the trees that are in the woods, The hol-ly bears the crown. The ris-ing of the sun,__ And the run-ning of the deer, The play-ing of the mer-ry or-gan, sweet sing-ing in the choir.

The holly bears a blossom
As white as the lily flower,
And Mary bore sweet Jesus Christ,
To be our sweet savior.

Refrain:
The rising of the sun,
And the running of the deer,
The playing of the merry organ,
Sweet singing in the choir.

The holly bears a berry,
As red as any blood,
And Mary bore sweet Jesus Christ,
To do poor sinners good.

The holly beats a prickle,
As sharp as any thorn,
And Mary bore sweet Jesus Christ,
On Christmas day in the morn.

Lute Book Lullaby

From William Ballet's Ms. Lute Book.

Anonymous

1. Sweet was the song the Vir - gin sang, When she to Beth - lem Ju - da came And was de - liv - ered of ___ a ___ son, That bless - ed Je - sus hath to name: Lul - la, lul - la, lul - la, lul - la-by, Lul - la, lul - la, lul - la, lul-la-by. 2. Sweet babe, sang she, my son, And eke a sav - ior born, Who has vouch -

saved from on high, To vis - it us that were for -

lorn, La-lu-la, la-lu-la la-lu-la - by, Sweet babe, sang

she And rocked him sweet - - ly on her knee.

Silent Night

Franz Grüber (1787–1863)

Silent night, holy night,
Shepherds quake at the sight.
Glories stream from heaven afar,
Heavenly hosts sing alleluia;
Christ our savior is born!
Christ our savior is born!

The Twelve Days of Christmas

Traditional

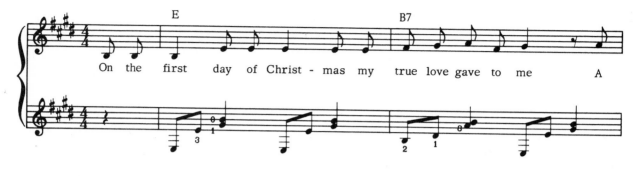

On the first day of Christ - mas my true love gave to me A

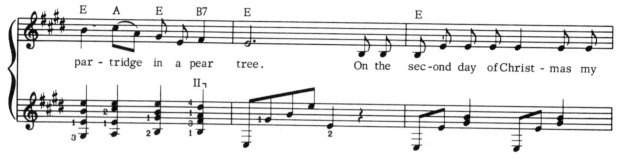

par - tridge in a pear tree. On the sec - ond day of Christ - mas my

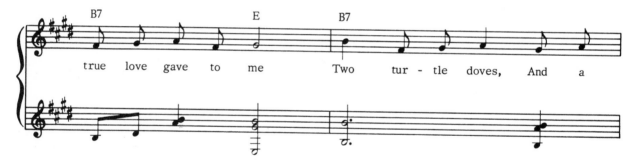

true love gave to me Two tur - tle doves, And a

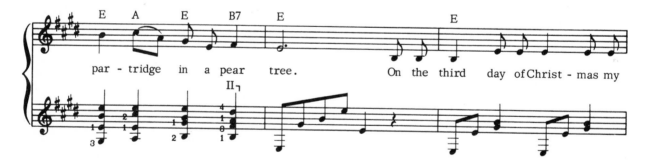

par - tridge in a pear tree. On the third day of Christ - mas my

true love gave to me Three french hens, Two tur - tle doves, And a

Two tur-tle doves, And a par-tridge in a pear tree.

On the sixth day of Christ - mas my true love gave to me
On the seventh day of Christ - mas my true love gave to me
On the eighth day of Christ - mas my true love gave to me
On the ninth day of Christ - mas my true love gave to me
On the tenth day of Christ - mas my true love gave to me
On the eleventh day of Christ - mas my true love gave to me
On the twelfth day of Christ - mas my true love gave to me

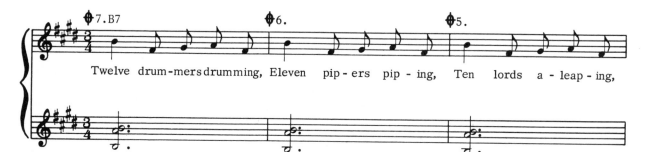

Twelve drum-mers drumming, Eleven pip-ers pip-ing, Ten lords a - leap-ing,

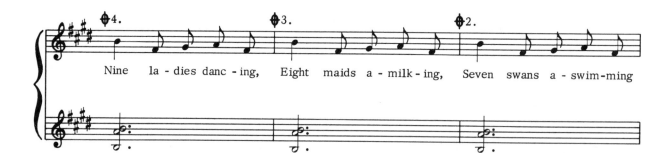

Nine la - dies danc - ing, Eight maids a - milk-ing, Seven swans a - swim-ming

Six geese a - lay-ing, Five gold-en__ rings, Four__ call - ing birds,

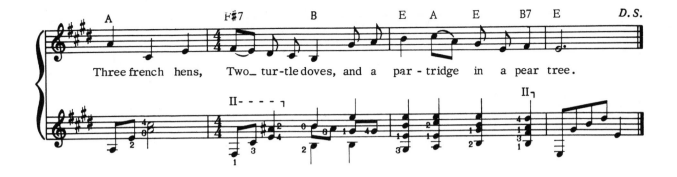

Three french hens, Two_ tur-tle doves, and a par-tridge in a pear tree.

We Three Kings

John Henry Hopkins (1820–1891)

Born a king on Bethlehem's plain,
Gold I bring to crown him again,
King forever, ceasing never,
Over us all to reign.

Refrain:
O star of wonder, star of night,
Star with royal beauty bright,
Westward leading, still proceeding,
Guide us to thy perfect light.

Frankincense to offer have I,
Incense owns a deity nigh;
Prayer and praising, all men raising,
Worship him God on high.

Myrrh is mine, its bitter perfume,
Breathes a life of gathering gloom:
Sorrowing, sighing, bleeding, dying,
Sealed in the stone cold tomb.

Glorious now behold him arise,
King and God and sacrifice;
Alleluia, alleluia,
Sounds through the earth and skies!

Art Songs

Abschied (Farewell)

Goethe

Mauro Giuliani (1781–1829)

Zu lieb - lich ist's, ein Wort zu brach - en, Zu schwer die woh - ler - kann - te
Was suchst du mir dich zu ver - steck - en! Sey of - fen, flieh___ nicht mein - en

Pflicht, Und lei - der kann man nichts ver - sprech - en, Was un - serm
Blick! Früh o - der spät musst' ichs' ent - deck - en, Und hier hast

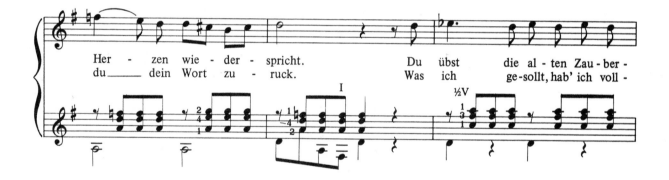

Her - zen wie - der - spricht. Du übst die al - ten Zau - ber -
du___ dein Wort zu - ruck. Was ich ge - sollt, hab' ich voll -

lie - der; Du___ lockst ihn der kaum ru - hig war, Zum Schauck - el -
en - det; Durch mich sey dir von nun an nichts ver - wehrt; Ver - zeih dem

80

kahn der süs-sen Thor-heit wie - der, Er-neust ver-dop - pelst die____ Ge-
Freund, der sich nun von dir wen-det, Und still in sich zu-ruc - ke-

fahr. Zum Schau-kel-kahn der süs-sen Thor-heit wie - der, Er-neust, ver-
kehrt. Ver-zeih dem Freund, der sich nun von dir wen - det. Und still in

dop - pelst die____ Ge-fahr.
sich zu-rüc - ke-kehrt.

Translation

Breaking one's promise is too easy,
Familiar duty is too hard.
Unfortunately we can promise nothing
Which contradicts our heart.
You chant the ancient magic spells,
You lure one who had just come to rest
Back to the tossing ship of folly,
And you renew and double the peril.

Why are you trying to hide from me?
Be open, do not flee my gaze!
Sooner or later I will discover it,
And then you'll get your promise back again
What I had to do, I accomplished;
From now on I will hinder you in nothing.
Forgive the friend who turns away
    from you,
And turns back quietly into himself.

Translation by Anne Goodrich Heck from Mauro Giuliani, Sechs Lieder Op. 89. *Tecla Editions, London.*

Belle Rose Porporine

Gabriello Chiabrera (1552–1638)   *Giulio Caccini (c. 1545–1618)*

di - te, Di bei den - ti cu - sto - di - te: _____
ri - re? Me mi - ran - do su'l mo - ri - re? _____

Verses 2 and 4.

2. Di - te, ro - se pre - zi - o - se, A - mo - ro - se, Di t'on -
4. Bel - le ro - se, o fe - ri - ta - te, O pie - ta - te, Del sì

d'è, _____ che s'io m'af - fi - so, Nel bel guar - do ac-ce - so ar -
far _____ la ca - gion si - a, Io vo' dir in nuo - vi

den - te Voi re - pen - te Di - scio - glie - te un bel sor -
mo - di Vos - tre lo - di, Ma ri - de - te tut - ta -

ri - so, Di - scio - glie - te un bel sor - ri - so? ri - so?_____
vi - a, Ma ri - de - te tut - ta - vi - a. vi - a._____

Translation

Fair purple roses,
Who amid thorns
Open not to the dawn,
But as ministers of Love
Protect the fair treasures
Of your beautiful teeth:

Say, precious, amorous rose,
How is that if I regard
Your ardent face
In a flash your smile
Comes forth?

Is it perhaps
To save my life
That cannot bear your disfavor,
Or is it that
You find pleasure
In seeing me perish?

Fair roses, whether
The reason is cruel or kind,
I will find new ways
To sing your praises
And you, continue to smile!

Come Again

John Dowland (1562–1626)

Come a - gain, sweet love doth now in - vite, Thy
Come a - gain, that I may cease to mourn, Through

grac - es that re - frain to do me due de - light.
thy un - kind dis - dain, for now left and for - lorn.

To see, to hear, to touch, to kiss, to die,___
I sit, I sigh, I weep, I faint, I die,___

With thee a - gain in sweet-est sym — pa - thy.
In dead-ly pain and end-less mis — er - y.

All the day the sun that lends me shine,
By frowns doth cause me pine,
And feeds me with delay:
Her smiles, my springs, that make my joys to grow,
Her frowns the winters of my woe.

All the night my sleeps are full of dreams,
My eyes are full of streams,
My heart takes no delight,
To see the fruits and joys that some do find,
And mark the storms are me assigned.

Out alas, my faith is ever true,
Yet will she never rue,
Nor yield me any grace:
Her eyes of fire, her heart of flint is made,
Whom tears nor truth may once invade.

Gentle Love draw forth thy wounding dart,
Thou canst not pierce her heart,
For I that do approve,
By sighs and tears more hot than are thy shafts,
Did tempt while she for triumph laughs.

Come, Sorrow, Come

Thomas Morley (1556–c1603)

Come,___ sor - row, come, sit down and mourn with me, Hang down thy head up -

on thy bale - ful breast, That God and man and all the world___

___ may see, Our hea - vy hearts do live in qui - et

rest.　　　　　En - fold thine　arms and wring and　wring thy wretch - ed

hands,　　　　　　　　To　show　the　state_____

____ where - in poor sor - row　stands,

To　show　the　state where - in poor sor - row　stands.

Cry not outright for that were childrens' guise,
But let thy tears fall trickling down thy face,
And weep so long until thy blubbered eyes,
May see (in Sun) the depth of thy disgrace.
Oh shake thy head, but not a word but mum.
The heart once dead, the tongue is
    stricken dumb.

And let our fare be dishes of despite,
To break our hearts and not our fasts withall,
Then let us sup with sorrow sops at night,
And bitter sauce, all of a broken gall;
Thus let us live, till heavens may rue to see,
The doleful doom ordained for thee and me.

Transcribed from the lute tablature by F. M. Noad

The Constant Lover

Sir John Suckling (1609–1642)   *Peter Heneker (1931–)*

Out up - on it! I have loved Three whole days to - ge - ther;
But the spite on't is, no praise Is due at all to me;___

And am like to love three more, If it prove fair wea - ther.
Love with me had made no stays, Had it not been she;

Time shall moult a - way his wings, Ere he shall dis - co - ver
Had it a - ny been but she, And that ve - ry face,___

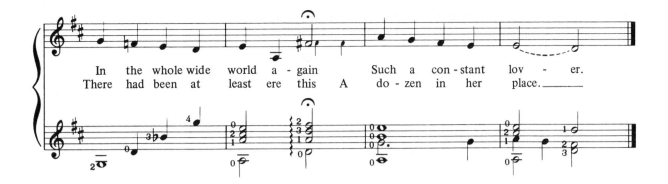

In the whole wide world a - gain   Such a con - stant lov - er.
There had been at least ere this   A do - zen in her place.

Go Chrystal Tears

John Dowland

to quick-en up   the thoughts of my de - sert,   which
Yet sighs and tears   to her   I sac - ri - fice   both

sleeps   too sound, whilst   I   from   her   de - part
from   a spot - less   heart   and   pa - tient   eyes

Have You Seen But A White Lily Grow?

Ben Jonson

Anonymous

soft,   O so sweet, So sweet,_____ so sweet   is   she.

Heiden-Röslein

Goethe

Franz Schubert (1797–1828)

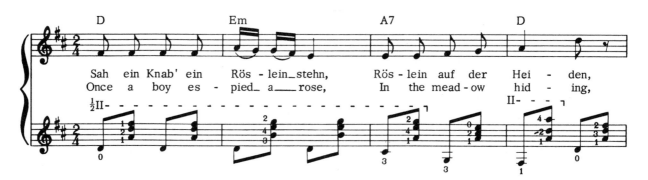

Sah ein Knab' ein Rös-lein stehn, Rös-lein auf der Hei - den,
Once a boy es - pied a rose, In the mead-ow hid - ing,

War so jung und mor-gen schön Lief er schnell es nah' zu sehn,
Morn-ing fresh its beau-ty such That the boy runs up to touch,

Sah's mit vie - len Freu - den, Rös-lein, Rös-lein, Rös-lein roth,
Joy his foot-steps guid - ing, Ros-lein, Ros-lein, Ros-lein red,

Rös - lein auf der Hei - den.
In the mead-ow hid - ing.

Knabe sprach: ich breche dich,
Röslein auf der Heiden!
Röslein sprach: ich steche dich,
Dass du ewig denkst an mich,
Und ich will's nicht leiden
Röslein, Röslein, Röslein roth,
Röslein auf der Heiden.

Und der wilde Knabe brach
Röslein auf der Heiden;
Röslein wehrte sich und stach,
Half ihm doch kein Weh' und Ach,
Musst' es eben leiden.
Röslein, Röslein, Röslein roth,
Röslein auf der Heiden.

Translation

"I will pluck thee," so says he;
In the meadow hiding,
But the rose replies in kind,
"Sharp's my thorn and you will find,
Your regret abiding."

Carelessly he plucks her forth,
In the meadow hiding.
Though her thorn would give him pain,
All her struggle is in vain;
Vain was all her chiding.

Röslein, Röslein, Röslein red,
In the meadow hiding.

Translation by F.M. Noad

Henry VIII's Song

Henry VIII

F. M. Noad

1. As the hol-ly grow-eth green, And nev-er chang-eth hue, So I am ev-er hath__ been Un-to my la - dy true. 2. As the hol-ly grow-eth green, With i-vy all a - lone, When__ flow-ers can not be seen And green-wood leaves be gone. 3. Now un - to my la - dy Pro-mise to her I make, From all oth-er__ on - ly To her I me__ be - take.

It Fell on a Summer's Day

Thomas Campian (1567–1620)

It fell on a sum-mer's day while sweet Bes-sy sleep-ing lay

In her bower___ on her bed, ___ Light with cur-tains shad - ow - ed,

Ja - mie came, She him spies, O-pening half her heav - y eyes.

Jamie stole in through the door,
She lay slumbering as before,
Softly to her he drew near;
She heard him, yet would not hear.
Bessy vowed not to speak,
He resolved that dump to break.

First a soft kiss he doth take,
She lay still and would not wake,
Then his hands learned to woo,
She dreamt not what he would do,
But still slept, while he smiled
To see love by sleep beguiled.

Jamie then began to play;
Bessy as one buried lay,
Gladly still through this sleight
Deceived in her own deceit;
And since this trance begun,
She sleeps every afternoon.

Arranged from the lute tablature by F.M. Noad

It Was A Lover and His Lass

William Shakespeare

Thomas Morley (1557–1602)

It was a lov-er and his lass, With a hey, and a ho, and a

hey no-ni - no, And a hey,_____ no-ni, no-ni - no.

That o'er the green corn-field did pass In spring-time, in

spring - time, In spring - time, the on-ly pret-ty ring time, When

birds do sing, hey ding-a-ding-a-ding, Hey ding-a-ding-a-ding, hey

Between the acres of the rye,
With a hey, and a ho, and a hey nonino,
And a hey, noni, nonino.
These pretty country folks would lie.

Refrain:
In springtime, in springtime,
In springtime, the only pretty ring time,
When birds do sing, hey ding-a-ding-a-ding,
Hey ding-a-ding-a-ding, hey ding-a-ding-a-ding,
Sweet lovers love the spring
In springtime, in springtime,
The only pretty ring time,
When birds do sing, hey ding-a-ding-a-ding,
Hey ding-a-ding-a-ding, hey ding-a-ding-a-ding,
Sweet lovers love the spring.

This carol they began that hour,
With a hey, and a ho, and a hey nonino,
And a hey, noni, nonino,
How that life was but a flower.

And therefore take the present time,
With a hey, and a ho, and a hey nonino,
And a hey, noni, nonino.
For love is crowned with the prime.

I Saw My Lady Weep

John Dowland (1562–1626)

Arranged from the lute tablature by F. M. Noad

full _____ of woe, But such a woe (be - lieve me) as wins more hearts
sighs _____ to sing, And all things with so sweet a sad - ness move
kills _____ the heart. O strive not to be ex - cel - lent in woe

Than mirth can do, with her, with her en - ti - cing charms.
As made my heart at once, at once both grieve and love.
Which on - ly breeds your beau - ty's o - ver throw.

103

The Lass with the Delicate Air

Michael Arne (1741–1786)

1. Young Molly who lives at the foot of the hill whose fame ev'ry virgin with envy does fill Of
2. One ev'ning last May, as I travers'd the grove, In thought-less retire-ments, not dream-ing of love I
3. That mo-ment young Cupid se-lect-ed a dart, And pierc'd with-out pi-ty my in-no-cent heart; From
4. A thou-sand times o'er I've re-peat-ed my suit, But still the tor-men-ter af-fects to be mute. Then

Passing By

Edward C. Purcell (d. 1932)

There is a la - dy sweet and kind, Was nev - er

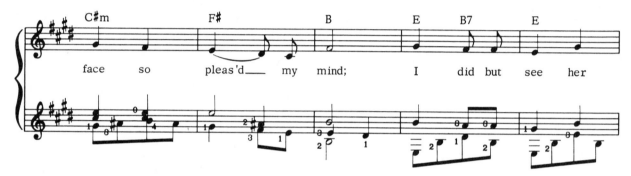

face so pleas'd my mind; I did but see her

pass - ing by, And yet I love her till I die.

Her gestures, motions and her smiles,
Her wit, her voice my heart beguiles,
Beguiles my heart, I know now why,
And yet I love her till I die.

Cupid is winged and doth range,
Doth range her country, so my love
  doth change,
But change the earth, or change the sky,
Yet will I love her till I die.

Pierrot's Song

Oliphant Down

F. M. Noad

Baby, don't wait for the moon,
She has scratched her white chin on
   the gorse;
And mellow and musical June
Is bringing the cuckoo remorse.

Baby, don't wait for the moon,
She is drawing the sea in her net;
And mellow and musical June
Is teaching the rose to forget.

Baby, don't wait for the moon,
The stairs of the sky are so steep;
And mellow and musical June
Is waiting to kiss you to sleep.

Plaisir D'Amour

Giovanni Martini (1706–1784)

Plai - sir d'a - - -

mour,_____ Ne du - re qu'un_ mo -

ment,_____ Cha - grin d'a - -

mour du - re tou - te la vi - - - -

e.

J'ai tout quit - té pour l'in grat - te Syl -

vi - - - e,_____

El - - le me quit - te et prend un au - - tre a -

mant.

109

Plai - sir d'a - mour, _____ Ne

du - - re qu'un___ mo - ment, _____ cha -

grin d'a - - mour du - re tou - te la___

vi - - - - e.

"Tant que cet-te eau cou - le - -

ra dou - ce - ment_____ Vers

ce ruis - seau qui bor - de la___ prai -

ri - e, Je t'ai - me -

rai, " Me ré - pé - tait___ Syl -

vi - e. L'eau cou - le_en -

core,____ El - le_a chan - gé____ pour -

tant.____

Plai - sir d'a - mour,____ Ne

du - re qu'un__ mo - ment,____ Cha -

grin   d'a — — mour   du – re   tou – te   la____

vi – – – – – – – e.

Que Ne Suis-Je La Fougère

C. H. Riboutté

Giovanni Battista Pergolesi (1710–1736)

Que ne suis – je la fou-
Would I were that glade of

gè - re Où, sur la fin___ d'un beau jour Se re-
fern trees As the sun falls be - low the hill Where a-

po - se ma ber - gè - re Sous la gar - de___ de l'a-
sleep lies my fair shep-herd-ess Guard-ed by fick - le Cu - pid's

mour.   Que ne suis – je le zé - phy - re Qui raf-
will.   Would I were the gen - tle zeph - yr That re-

fraî – chit ses ap - pas L'air que sa bou - che res-
fresh – es her re - treat Or the air her lips are

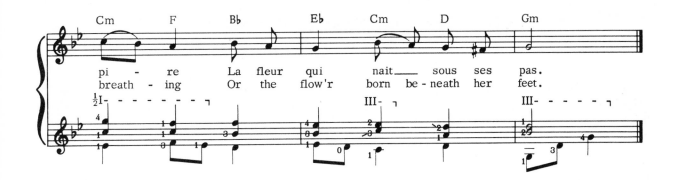

pi - re La fleur qui nait____ sous ses pas.
breath - ing Or the flow'r born be - neath her feet.

The Self-Banished

Dr. John Blow (1649–1708)

It is not that___ I love you less___ than when___ be --
fore___ your feet I lay; But to pre - vent___ the
sad in - crease of hope - less___ love___ I keep a - way
In vain a - las for - ev - 'ry - thing · which I___ have___
known___ be - longs___ to you, Your form does to___ my___

fan - cy bring and makes my old wounds bleed a - new.

Serenade (*Ständchen*)

English version by Henry G. Chapman

Franz Schubert (1797–1828)

1. Lei - se fleh - en mei - ne lie - der durch die Nacht zu
1. Soft - ly goes my song's en-treat - y, Through the night to

dir,
thee,

In __ den stil - len Hain __ her - nie - der, Lieb - chen Komm zu
In __ the si - lent woods I wait thee, Come my love __ to

mir.
me.

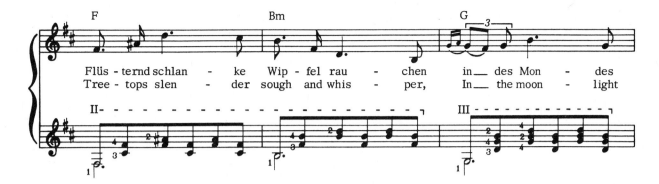

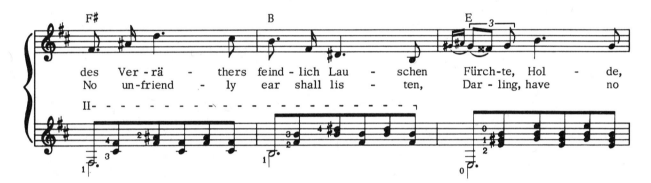

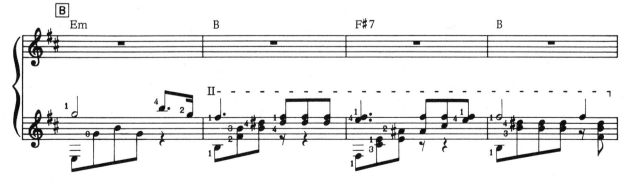

119

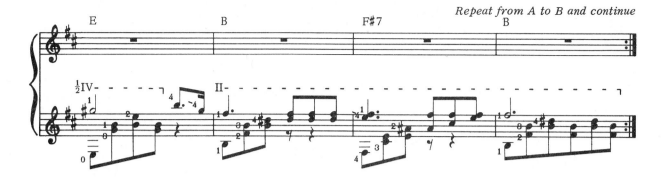

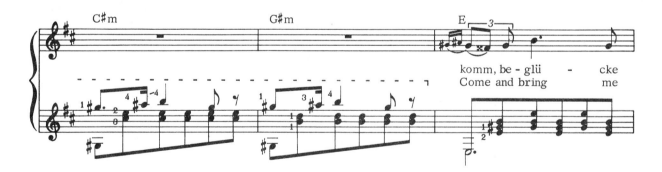

120

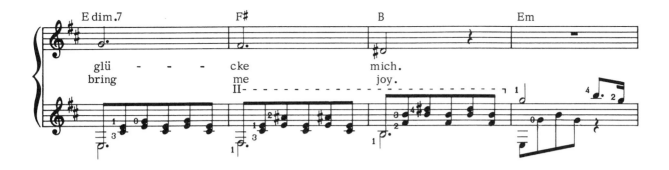

glü — — — cke mich.
bring me joy.

Hörst die Nachtigallen schlagen? Ach! sie
    flehen dich,
Mit der Töne süssen Klagen flehen sie
    für mich.
Sie versteh'n des Busens Sehnen, Kennen
    Liebesschmerz,
Kennen Liebesschmerz, rühren mit den
    Silbertönen jedes
Weiche Herz, jedes weiche Herz.

Lass auch dir die Brust bewegen, Liebchen,
    höre mich!
Bebend harrich dir entgegen, komm,
    beglücke mich!
Komm, beglücke mich, beglücke mich.

Sigh No More, Ladies
(from *Much Ado About Nothing*)

William Shakespeare (1564–1616)

F. M. Noad

Sigh no more, la - dies, sigh ___ no more Men were de -
Then sigh ___ not so, but let ___ them go, And be you

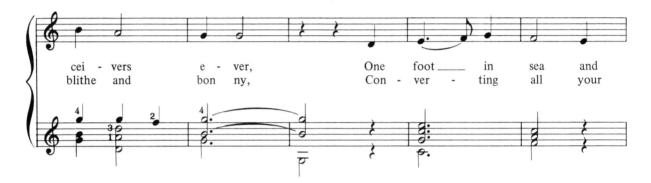

cei - vers e - ver, One foot ___ in sea and
blithe and bon - ny, Con - ver - ting all your

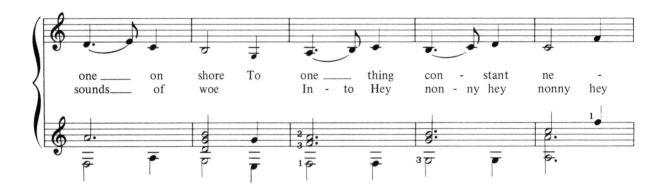

one ___ on shore To one ___ thing con - stant ne -
sounds ___ of woe In - to Hey non - ny hey nonny hey

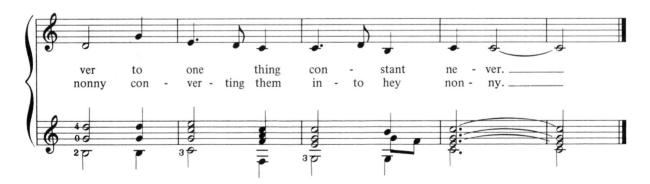

ver to one thing con - stant ne - ver. ___
nonny con - ver - ting them in - to hey non - ny. ___

Sing no more ditties, sing no more,
Of dumps so dull and heavy;
The fraud of men was ever so,
Since summer first was leafy:
Then sigh not so, but let them go,
And be you blithe and bonny,
Converting all your sounds of woe
Into Hey nonny, nonny.

Si La Noche Haze Escura

16th Century Villancico

1. Si la no - che ha-ze es-cu - ra ha-
4. Há - ze me vi - vir pe - na -

ze es-cu - ra y tan cor - to es
- - da y mués - tra - se

el ca - mi - no Có - mo no ve nis có - mo
me e - ne - mi - go Có - mo no ve - nis có - mo

fine

no ve - ni - - s a - mi - go.
no ve - ni - - s a - mi - go.

2. La me - dia no - che es pass - a - -
3. Mi des - di - cha lo de tie - -

da   Y el   que me pe - na   no vie - -
ne   que nas-ci tan des-di-cha da, que nas-ci tan des-di-cha

D.C.

- ne no vie - ne no vie - ne
- da tan des - - di cha - da.

Translation

Since the night is dark
And the road is so short
Why do you not come my friend?
Midnight is past,
And he who torments me comes not,
My luckless fate keeps him away,
The fate that I was born to,
Makes me live in grief,
And fortune is my foe,
Why do you not come my friend?

Arranged by F. M. Noad

125

Sleep Wayward Thoughts

John Dowland (1562–1626)

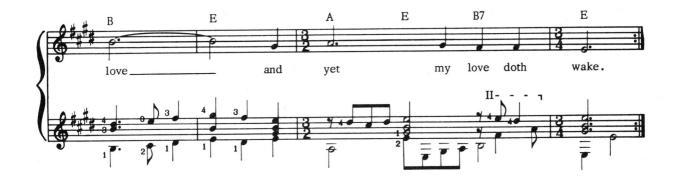

love _____ and yet my love doth wake.

My love doth rage,
And yet my love doth rest
Fear in my love, and yet my love secure.
Peace in my love, and yet my love oppressed,
Impatient, yet of perfect temp'rature.
Sleep dainty love, while I sigh for thy sake.
So sleeps my love and yet my love doth wake.

Song at Nightfall (Aftonkväde)
Fredman's Song No. 32

English words F. M. Noad

Carl Michael Bellman (1740–1795)

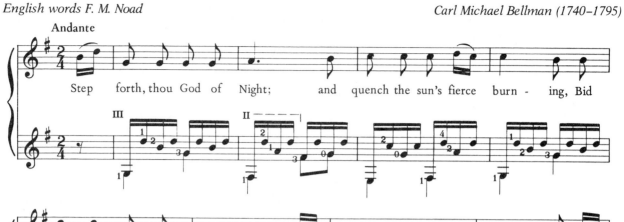

Step forth, thou God of Night; and quench the sun's fierce burn - ing, Bid

thou the eve - ning star her gen - tle light be turn - ing To

pierce the twi - light sky, Cool now the heat - ed wave, and

pas - sion's fie - ry yearn - ing, Now veil the languo - rous eye.

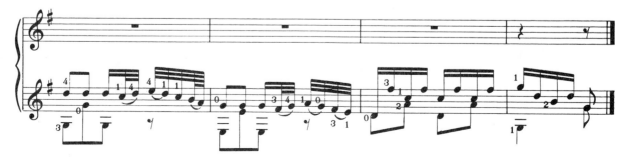

See Flora's courtyards fair, her beauteous
  hilltops flying,
While there the somber tombs in darker hills
  are lying,
Thy cloak conceals them all.
From secret lairs come forth moles, snakes,
  and martens flying,
To hear the screech-owl's call.

Soft Zephyrs stir the leaves, and in the
  forest shade
Blue water darkly flows, reflecting through
  the glade
The rower's glistening oar.
Where drifting currents merge the greedy
  pike, displayed,
Leaps 'gainst the rock once more.

The river dweller now by moon's half light
  is seen,
Atop the flowery bank, that spans the stretch
  between
His garden and the silt.
His water pitcher filled, his plot so neat
  and green
Is silvered now, and gilt.

Now rests the silent lark, her leafy bower
  filling,
And through the field of rye the blackbird's
  note is trilling
To cricket's harsh refrain
The swallow, freed by Pan, to serve his master
  willing
Flies low to warn of rain.

Arachne stay your hand and let your
  needle rest,
Can you resist the lyre, and steel your
  tender breast
Against Apollo's blow?
Lay Vulcan down your sledge, let hand to
  brow be pressed
As I to slumber go.

Strike The Viol

Henry Purcell (1659–1695)

Strike   the   Vi - ol,

Strike   the   Vi - ol,   Touch,   touch,   touch,   touch,

touch,   touch   the Lute;   Wake   the   Harp,

Wake   the   Harp,   Wake   the   Harp,   In -

Arranged from the figured bass by F. M. Noad

130

spire the Flute; Wake the Harp, In -

spire the Flute; Sing your Pa - tro - nes - s's

Praise, Sing your Pa - tro - nes - s's Praise, Sing,

sing, sing, sing in cheer - - - - -

- - - - - - full and Har - mon - nious Lays.

Tant Que Vivray

Clément Marot

Claude de Sermisy (c. 1490–1562)

1. Tant que viv - ray, en â - ge flo - ris - sant,
2. Par plu - sieurs jours m'a te - nu lan - guis - sant,

Je ser - vi - rai d'a - mour le dieu puis - sant
Mais a - prés deuil m'a fait re - jou - is - sant,

En faits, en dicts, _____ en chan - sons et ac - cords.
Car j'ai l'a - mour _____ de la bel - le au gent corps.

3. Son al - li - an - ce c'est ma fi - an - ce, son couer est mien,

Le mien est sien, fi de tris - tes - se, vi - ve li - es - se,

Puis - qu'en a - mour, puis - qu'en a - mour a _____ tant de biens.

Translation

As long as I live and flourish
I will serve the powerful god of love
In word and deed, in song and harmony.

For several days he caused me to languish
But after sorrow came rejoicing
Since the fair limbed beauty loves me.

To be joined with her is my pledge
Her heart is mine.
Mine is hers, let sorrow give place to
    happiness,
For the joys of love are many.

Transcribed from the Attaigant lute version by F. M. Noad

Ungeduld (Impatience)

Wilhelm Müller

Franz Schubert (1797–1828)

Rather fast

1. Ich schnitt' es gern in al - le
2. Ich möcht' mir zie - hen ei - nen
3. Den Mor - gen-win - den möcht' ich's
4. Ich meint', es müsst' in mei - nen

Rin - den ein, Ich grüb' es gern in je - den Kie - sel-stein, Ich
jun - gen Star, Bis dass er spräch' die Wor - te rein und klar, Bis
hau - chen ein, Ich möcht' es säu - seln durch den re - gen Hain; O,
Au´ - gen stehn, Auf mei - nen Wan - gen müsst' man's bren - nen sehn, Zu

möcht' es sän auf je - des fri - sche Beet   Mit Kres-sen-sa-men, der es
er sie spräch' mit mei - nes Mun - des Klang,   Mit mei - nes Her - zens vol - lem,
leuch - tet es aus je - dem Blu - men-stern!   Trüg' es der Duft zu ihr von
le - sen wär's auf mei - nem stum - men Mund,   Ein je - der A - tem-zug gäb's

Translation

Would I could carve it on the trunk of every tree,
And engrave it on every stone,
Would I could sow it into each fresh flowerbed
With seeds of cress that would fast reveal it:
"My heart is thine, and will be so for ever."

Would I could teach a young starling,
Until it spoke the words, simple and clear,
Until it spoke with my own voice,
And the passion of my full heart;
Then could he sing through her window:
"My heart is thine, and will be so for ever."

Would I could breathe it to the morning breeze,
And whisper it through the lively woods,
O could it radiate from every bloom!
And could their scent bring it to you from near and far!
You waves, can you drive nought but the mill-wheel?
"My heart is thine, and will be so for ever."

I thought, it must show in my eyes,
The burning of my cheeks must show,
It must be there to read from my silent mouth,
And there to hear from every breath;
Yet she sees nothing of my fearful anguish:
"Thine is my heart, and will be so for ever."

What Then Is Love But Mourning?

Philip Rosseter (c 1575–1623)

What then is love but mourn - ing? What de - sire but a self burn - ing? 'Till she that hates doth love re - turn, Thus will I mourn, thus will I sing:. Come a - way, Come a - way, my dar - ling.

Beauty is but a blooming,
Youth in his glory entombing.
Time hath a while which none can stay.
Then come away
While thus I sing:
Come away, come away, my darling.

Summer in winter fadeth;
Gloomy night heavenly light shadeth;
Like to the morn are Venus' flowers,
Such are her hours.
Then will I sing:
Come away, come away, my darling.

136

Where'er You Walk

William Congreve

G. F. Handel (1685–1759)

Trees, where you sit, Shall crowd in - to a__ shade,____ ____

____ ____ ____ Trees where you__ sit,

ad lib.   *a tempo*

Shall crowd____ in - to____ a shade.

Fine

Where - 'er you tread, The blush - ing flow'rs shall rise, And

all   things flour-ish, And all   things flour-ish,   Where -

D. C. al Fine

'er you turn your eyes,   Where -'er you turn your eyes, where-'er you   turn your eyes.

The Willow Song

William Shakespeare (From Othello)

Anonymous

A poor soul sat sigh - ing By a sy - ca-more tree; Sing all a green__ wil - low, With his hand on his bos - om, And his head____ on his knee, Oh wil - low, wil - low, wil - low, wil - low, Oh wil - low, wil - low, wil - low, wil - low, My gar - land shall

He sighed in his singing
And made a great moan,
I am dead to all pleasure
My true love she is gone.

Refrain:
Oh willow, willow, willow, willow,
Oh, willow, willow, willow, willow,
My garland shall be;
Sing all a green willow,
Willow, willow, willow,
Sing all a green willow,
My garland shall be.

The mute bird sat by him
Was made tame by his moans.
The true tears fell from him
Would have melted the stones.

Come all you forsaken
And mourn you with me,
Who speaks of a false love
Mine's falser than she.

Appendix

COMMON CHORD CHART

MAJOR

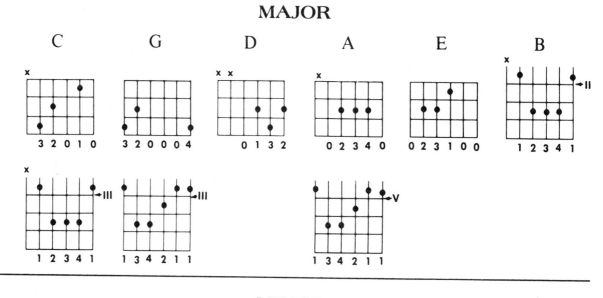

MINOR

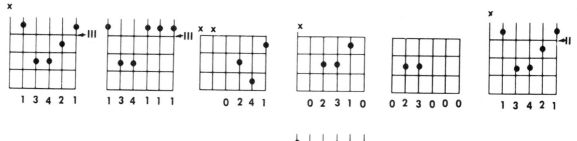

SEVENTH

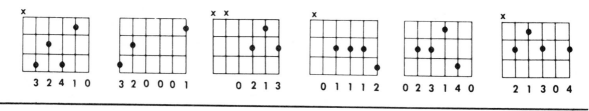

DIMINISHED

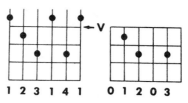

Roman numerals show behind which fret to place your bar.

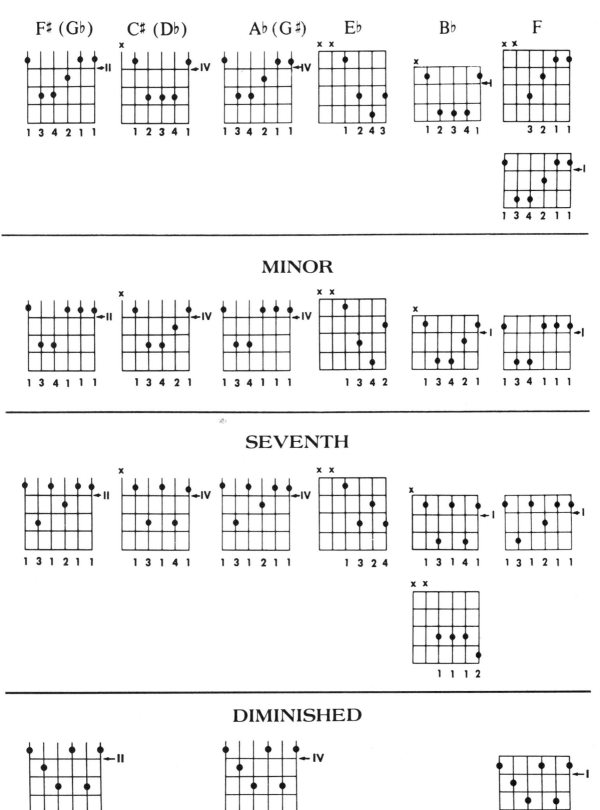

145

Index

Title Index

First Line Index